Welcome To The Red

SOLID STARTUPS

101 Solid Business Ideas

By

SCOTT MCDOWELL

101 BIZ IDEAS 2019

MOSTLY FREE TO START LOW SKILL

AND SCALABLE BUSINESSES

TIME TESTED AND NO HYPE!!

Table of Contents

STARTING A BUSINESS

I hope this book helps you find a simple start up idea, Replicate the winners that already exist, and get rich.

You can try out lots of businesses for next to nothing, start them up, shut them down within days and weeks rather than months and years.

There are no guarantees for success in life and business so you will have to find what works for you, test, experiment and adapt. I hope this book gives you some ideas, inspires you and gives you the courage to move forward.

Even if you do not use the business ideas in this book it will help you think of ways to start other projects.

Find something easy that you know you can do, stick with it and scale it.

Build the business, hire good employees and make some real money this year.

K.I.S.S. Keep it simple stupid.

Anyone can do it, and dont let anyone tell you otherwise.

NUMBER 1 -
WEDDING PLANNING

Im sure you know how expensive weddings can be, the average wedding in the U.K costs around £20,000 and as a wedding planner you can charge 10-20% of the total cost of the wedding.

You can create a template for all the weddings to work from, and even offer a set price for a simple repeatable option using all your own reusable furnishings for the template wedding option.

If you take the initiative to have your own videographer, photographer and catering etc this becomes an extremely lucrative business, as all these services are usually sold seperately at prices you could easily compete with, if you sell a full-service package that takes care of everything for the customer.

Starting this business cost's you nothing as everything is available to be supplied by other businesses, and you can order everything you need with the deposit you receive or full payment when the customer decides to use your service.

With so many add on profit centres like cake making and dress rental services, you can see the opportunity can keep growing if you can organise hire and reinvest into multiple services within your industry.

NUMBER 2 -

POWER WASHING

Have you ever thought about the startup cost for this business, you can rent, pay in installments or borrow a power washer and you are in business.

What will you or your employees be doing? washing down drive ways, houses and roofs occasionally.

No education needed with this one, if you have one good arm and you can point at dirt, your in business.

I am guessing your thinking this is a low paying job considering the skill level, but no it will cost you anywhere from $60-100 per hour in the U.S.A. how does $800 dollars a day sound to you?

You don't even need to have any marketing cost at first, you can try door to door sales if you have the will to do it.

Once you have made some money from starting your venture, you can reinvest it into more elaborate set ups, for quick use when travelling by van.

You can offer a sample clean of part of the driveway if the customer is on the fence about taking you up on your service.

Offer other services to help fill up your calendar if you have trouble getting bookings in your area. Always experiment!

NUMBER 3 -

CARPET CLEANING

This business requires you to buy or rent a high quality steam or dry cleaning machine you will also need the correct type of detergent for the type of carpets you may encounter, so do your homework before rushing in.

The skill level for this job is fairly low and you can charge around $80-130 to clean a house just 200 to 400 square feet in size.

It is similar in some ways to the power washing business and could be another business to work at the same time.

You will need a van to transport the cleaner and hold all your chemicals which is another expense to consider.

Most companies lease their vehicles, it might be worth asking your accountant for advice on this as there may be tax incentives in certain circumstances.

In the future you may want to buy the carpet cleaning machines to lower your expenses in the coming years.

You should set up a google my business account, and learn how to manage it correctly for more bookings and helpful features. There are youtube tutorials that help guide and advise you through this amazing marketing platform for your local businesses.

NUMBER 4 -

WOOD FLOORING SANDING AND

POLISHING

This is another business that is similar to the power washing and carpet cleaning, and when combined compliments and expands your opportunities. It also helps you cut costs on advertising if you have complimentary businesses that can be advertised together.

You will need a commercial sander and a hand sander to get right into the corners of the wood flooring. Like the other businesses mentioned you can rent or buy the machine in full or in instalments. You will need rollers and paint brushes for varnishing the flooring after sanding.

It will be a lot easier if you have a van to carry around the machinery needed.

If you decide to buy a van consider buying something a couple of years old but with low mileage, no one cares how old your van is and you can save a lot of money buying used rather than new.

The Pricing for this service varies a lot from country to country and state to state, an average of $40 to $70 per sq metre is likely in the U.S. for sanding and polishing.

NUMBER 5 -
PET GROOMING

If you love dogs this is a great job for you and a great business that is in demand and in some areas under supplied.

Supply and demand is one of the basic fundamentals to watch when evaluating any business, so research as best you can.

A good way to find out how great a demand for a service is, by asking your competitors how soon can I get booked in, if it's an unreasonable amount of time, your in luck!

The tools of the trade are very much like a barbers for pet grooming.

You will need clippers, scissors and a few large bowls or a commercial size washing up sink.

Set up as if your going to be busy in the future with every process the dogs go through in order and in one direction just like a line would be in manufacturing, or a good commercial kitchen with each work place next to its logical successor.

I would watch many training videos, practice on my own pets, and possibly get some training or work for someone else if you don't feel confident in your ability to do a good job. You want to get great reviews and have as much repeat custom as possible just like any other business.

Pet groomers usually charge between $40-75 depending on the size of the dog.

NUMBER 6 -

CAMERA MAN/VIDEOGRAPHY

I know what your thinking I didn't go to film school and I don't think Steven Spielberg is going to hire me, your right this is not about movies, this is about weddings, birthday parties, advertising videos, events and more.

It requires very little start up cost and skills, get yourself a decent camera, these days you can get a great camera for less than $100 you can record sporting activities on a gopro with no problem, they were made by a surfer for shooting footage while surfing.

Look into what is required for your type of camera business. There are lots of videos on youtube that help you with your camera skills.

There are great video templates available that are easy to use like Envato and Renderforest, to help make your final product look amazing for your customers. You can keep pushing the boundaries of your editing skills as long as your in business, and seperate yourself from all the competition with your own unique style and execution.

The average hire cost per wedding is 1-3 thousand dollars $$$

NUMBER 7 -

INTERIOR DESIGNER

A service business that has no set up cost but has great potential for you.

If you understand or you can simply follow the concepts in the interior design field then apply them to your customers project.

Hiring an interior designer costs on average $2000 to $5000 but you can make your own pricing strategy that works for your company.

In some countries you need to take an exam to be able to call yourself an interior designer, although nothing stops you from starting a business and having interior designers work for you, problem solved.

If it sounds scary hiring interior designers to work for you dont worry, you can first work on seeing how many leads you can generate, by advertising with a facebook lead ad and see if you can get enough leads before you commit to hiring anyone.

Then you can hire someone on a trial basis alleviating most of the risk associated with hiring, as you only have to come up with the first months salary which you should be able to cover from all the leads we have generated.

If you have the knowledge and planning skills required, you have a great chance for success.

NUMBER 8 -

PARTY DECORATOR

This is a fun business for someone to start, setting up themed party decorations and centre pieces that turn the average party in to an event for your customers and their friends to enjoy.

The cost to start this business will obviously vary and spending a little more might pay off for you by giving customers a great night that all the party goers will remember and talk about for months. All the guests for the party are free advertising for your company if you create something memorable and conversation worthy.

It could be worth asking customer if its ok to leave some business cards on some of the tables where your best work is being displayed.

You will need to acquire things like projectors and mannequins you can dress up, chair covers and anything entertaining you can think of that will help you stand out and get repeat bookings.

The average price to get a decorator is between $700 and $1100 with expenses being just labour and the one-time cost of decorations.

Life rewards effort, so make it as special as you can imagine.

NUMBER 9 -
PEST CONTROL

This is a much-needed service which helps maintain the health of us all by stopping certain animals that carry disease from interacting with our food supply.

Unfortunately, you will have to kill some animals usually mice and rats with poison, but the main job is really keeping them out in the first place, filling the gaps they enter from and stopping them pursuing your client's premises in the first place.

This is another business that you need licensed workers for, it's worth looking into your state or countries laws before trying to start this business.

Tasks you have to carry out are not for the squeamish, after laying traps and laying out boxes of poison you will encounter dead animals daily.

The best part of the pest control business is the subscription-based model, for the most part you're billing your clients monthly even though there may be very little to do most of the year.

The monthly subscription averages at $43, you can multiply by your possible customer base per month to have a guess at your future sales, or just for the fun of seeing how the numbers add up.

NUMBER 10 -

PERSONAL ASSISTANT SERVICES

Create a personal assistant service that is flexible, in person or virtual assistants with the resources of a team rather than just an individual freelancer.

Another service-based business with little to no start-up cost and a very flexible set of services you can offer. Personal assistants do tasks such as diary management and taking care of travel arrangements and any other day to day tasks possible.

The average Virtual assistant in the U.S.A. earns around $30 to $50 an hour.

There is a lot of competition from overseas for virtual assistants, so I would consider creating a higher end in person P.A. business to distinguish yourself from everyone else.

This service is becoming more popular with the average person rather than just business owners, executives and celebrities with the understanding that any hour you work might be more valuable than the amount you would be able to pay someone to do these types of tasks.

For example: You only have one hour in the day after all your work and responsibilities. You can make $40 by working an extra hour on Ebay and have your personal assistant working for you for $30 an hour doing other work-related tasks, you have made $10 extra.

You would have lost $10 if you had done the tasks the personal assistant did.

P. A's sell the value of time and money.

NUMBER 11 -
CHILD CARE

If you're going into this business to make money you cant play small and take care of a small number of children and expect to make a lot. The average child carer in the U.S. only makes around $20,000 per year.

The other downside to this business is there is a lot of regulations to follow and paperwork that comes with it.

If you have the patience with all the regulations and you have a good mind for buying and scaling businesses you can create something on a large scale, as these businesses actually need to be everywhere that working parents exist.

Child care costs have always been high and differ massively from place to place. There will always be a need for this service so you do not have to worry about whether this will be around in the next ten or 20 years due to technological advancements.

With population increases in your location comes new mothers and fathers needing your services, it might be worth considering whether your local population is increasing or decreasing. Make sure that young people are not moving away from your town as that is your market for new customers in the future, you want child bearing aged adults moving into your town in the ideal scenario.

This is a highly needed and evergreen business.

NUMBER 12 –

TREE SURGEON

If you start this business you can tell people you're a surgeon, I'm guessing a brain surgeon is not very happy with that but this is an extra perk of the job. Tree surgery does require specialist knowledge, as you are working with biological systems.

Tasks include cutting down trees (tree felling) stump grinding, garden clearance and other similar tasks. The work involves power tools and climbing so can be dangerous for the absent minded. Insurance will be vital for your employees.

Tree surgeons earn £40 an hour on average in the U.K. but don't seem to earn a very high salary. Maybe this is due to low demand which should be made up with other outdoor services such as landscaping and other gardening services.

When you have a business with a low demand your marketing and branding skills should become extremely important to you. Also, you should consider covering larger territories to make up for the lack of demand in your particular area.

You should definitely have a version of your business branding exclusively aimed at Tree Surgery so you stand out as the expert in that niche rather than a generalist landscaping and garden services provider.

To keep costs down make use of online advertising, using face book fan pages, free websites and google my business.

NUMBER 13 –

CUSTOM CAKES

If you want to make a lot of money in the cake business just make that extra bit of mental effort, use creativity then adapt, and copy some of the amazing cake makers doing things at the highest level.

The level of customisation to your customers needs and wants will determine a lot of your success. You will need to guide and show examples of what is possible with your services.

Anything from 3D printing figures of your favourite celebrity to the birthday boy himself is now possible. And the wow factor of these custom cakes with the base of the cakes being more like a landscape of your favourite place in life or entertainment makes it possible to sell your products for massive profits.

The start up cost and skill level might be a barrier to entry for some, but the rewards could be worth it especially if you're willing to try out new types of creative processes which will lead to you standing seperately from the generic cake suppliers most towns have.

The top end cakes sell for tens of thousands of dollars, especially the wedding cakes that almost everyone that has ever got married has paid a fortune for.

I wonder how much someone would pay for a tiered wedding cake that shows the journey of their relationship in stages up to the wedding day.

NUMBER 14 -

YOGA STUDIO

Yoga and meditation has become normal and you can jump on the trend that is going to be here, probably forever.

They say stress is a killer, so teaching this ancient practise that is scientifically proven to lower stress levels among other things is more than just a social and entertaining activity for your community.

If your thinking, i'm only an amateur at Yoga and I don't feel I can justify teaching, that's ok. Your job as the business owner is to hire a great all weather venue where you can offer 1 hour Yoga classes all day and hire good teachers to teach your students.

The average price per session in the U.S. is $12 but can be much higher in some studios. The number of clients you can attract and the premium you can charge for a better brand, service and scenic location can make all the difference.

Consider opening early and closing late.

Always consider ways of leveraging other peoples businesses and groups that already posses your target audience. If you have a sport centre that does not offer Yoga you can ask to hire out part of this space to take advantage of the clientele that already exists, saving you most of the advertising costs for setting up on your own premises.

Large hotels and spas are another way to use an existing customer base to your advantage.

NUMBER 15 –

IRONING SERVICE

Dry cleaning businesses have created a lot of millionaires and maybe you could be the next if you follow in the their footsteps.

If you don't have the start up capital to start buying the dry cleaning machines, you can start by just offering an ironing service which only requires you having irons and ironing boards.

You can offer delivery at a cost which will help you pay for the leasing of your van.

Using part of your home or cheap commercial unit can save you money, but also consider a shop in a residential area to take advantage of the customers already using the other stores, next door to the supermarket would be ideal.

Dont just sell a product when you can create a great offer, this is a mistake most businesses make. Could you offer a great membership offer to keep your customers with you for more than just a one off service, and get paid every month without fail on a recurring basis. How quickly will a great offer make you the leader of your industry or location.

Ironing is not glamorous but its a great business and has made many millionaires all over the world, look for highly populated and affluent areas if possible.

NUMBER 16 –

KITCHEN FITTING

If you like DIY especially the easier carpentry tasks and furniture assembly this could be for you.

You can find training courses that teach kitchen fitting in most cities and anything you cant do can be sub contracted to a different business.

Considering the simplicity of most of the kitchen installation process, you are getting paid very well for your time.

Kitchen installation probably averages at about £2000 in the U.K. and takes about a days work for 2 men to install an average sized kitchen, you can do the math.

If you dont have the money for the tools you can always hire them, get yourself going then invest in buying them further down the road.

You can practise on 2 cabinets if you have the space in the garage or a similar space taking them apart and putting them back together, buy one piece of laminate worktop to practise joining the worktops together which is the most intricate work you will have to perform.

An easy way to get these jobs for free is calling up other trades men who offer different services, and offering them a commision for each referall, this way you only pay for advertising when you actually get a job booked.

NUMBER 17 -
SERVICED ACCOMODATION

Im sure you have heard of the company airbnb, for those of you who have not it's a site that helps you rent out your spare rooms and any other rental property you own by the night, turning your place into a room rental service.

If you can get the bookings you can make more money charging by the night than renting your property by the week or month. If you have a rental property and can get someone to take care of all the service aspect, you should at least try this first and see if you can generate enough bookings to make it worth renting out in this way. Always take new expenses into account.

You don't have to use airbnb but they are the most successful room sharing service at this point in time. There are other services that cater to particular niches like tradesmen or businessmen.

Renting out one of your own rooms is a really easy way to start making money this week with no start up capital needed. Maybe locks on the bedroom doors and a new set of keys for the guests if necessary.

If you have a quircky property dont be put off by that, its still worth a try as it will cost you nothing for the experiment. One of the most popular types of housing for serviced accomodation is the tree houses because of the novelty factor that it has, novelty can be a differentiating factor that sets you apart from the crowd and brings in the customers.

NUMBER 18 -
LIMO SERVICE

Well let's state the obvious, its just a really long car, usually offered to drive around party goers or small groups needing transport.

To stand out from the crowd you could wrap the limo to create a unique looking vehicle rather than blend in with the competition.

Start up costs include rental, lease or purchase instalments, insurance and road tax.

To hire a Limo costs between $65-190 per hour and it costs even more for a party bus which is something else to consider. Weddings and funerals obviously get a lot of bookings so a busy church is a good target for referall business and promotion.

You could do a deal with night clubs offering a package where it picks up the customer and drops them off at the vip line adding to the prestige and excitement of their customers evening.

In between your bookings you can turn on your uber or lyft app and start working so you dont have any wasted hours in the vehicles.

Airport runs working with taxi firms if they can not fulfill their customers needs may be another option to consider.

NUMBER 19 -

CREATE A YOUTUBE CHANNEL

I could talk all day about this but let's keep this simple. The opportunity to make video content of yourself in whatever niche you think you can make an impact is available to you for free, and the viewership continues to grow each year.

Dont worry about tech to much, if you own a decent phone that was made in the last few years, you have more than enough to get started with youtube. It will be to your benefit to invest in better equipment, especially for the sound quality.

Look at the channels and videos that are getting lots of views, learn from and emulate them. The titles and the thumbnail picture are of massive importance when it comes to views. The Click bait titles still work and the top youtubers copy each others titles all the time, usually with slight tweaks to look different from another channel.

We live in a world where people make millions from reviewing toys and gadgets, doing make up tutorials and other how to videos, playing computer games and messing with their friends in front of a phone camera. At least get a little piece of this digital money pie for yourself.

Have a look at social blade to see estimated earnings for channels you like, its not a perfect way to find out how much some channels are earning but it gives you an idea.

Make money with Ad revenue, consulting, selling products and services, sponsorships and lots more.

NUMBER 20 –

CAR FLIPPING

Buy and sell cars for profit, this is great if you have skills and experience in mechanics.

The simplest way to do this is find a car selling below the market value and sell it on, if you can find someone looking for a particular car to add to their collection it can be exceptionally profitable, rather than just putting a price up online for someone to find.

Car's that are selling cheap and need simple fixes are great opportunities.

Green cars and ugly coloured cars sell for less, you can get these wrapped and sell them at a higher price.

If you're good at restoring and improving cars you will make money with this strategy, working in a garage will make you money, but controlling an asset like a car and renovating for profit can make you a lot more, especially when you find the right cars.

Like everything you invest your money in, you will have to do the research when looking into each opportunity and have the guts to take action before you miss your chance.

If you reinvest your capital wisely you will be restoring classic luxury vehicles that can make you exceptional profits, and get you featured in magazines and online channels that are looking for that next story and help you promote your latest project.

NUMBER 21 –

WHOLESALE PRODUCTS FOR CAR

BOOT SALE/FLEA MARKET

Why try selling in these types of venues, because the cost of opening your store front is so cheap and that gives you more money to test different products and find out what you should really be selling.

Where should you buy your wholesale products? For return on investment your probably going to want to at least look at alibaba or go to salehoo to find hundreds of wholesale suppliers in the U.S.

You can use google trends to find trending products or look at everyday items that sell really well. Don't get stuck on any product or niche, test, test, test until you win. Start up cost is up to you, if your willing to buy from Alibaba it might be lower than expected.

This is good if you hate technology and dont want to get into the ecommerce space at all.

When you find your profitable niche and products you can employ someone to work at the next flea market or open your first stand or a store in the mall. Your highest probability of succeeding in the next store is by doing the same thing with the same type of customers, so replicating what your doing with the flea markets is a very good bet.

Its better to have 1 profitable flea market stand than a thousand stores that barely break even because of all the rent, taxes and maintenance, why not go for 1000 stands instead.

NUMBER 22 -

FOOD TRUCK

If you have an idea for a restaurant or fast food business one of the easiest ways to try it out is by using a food truck.

Renting a truck can cost around $2-3000 a month and there can be other costs to consider as well, such as parking permits or getting a site at an event.

Insurance, tax, product costs.

The good thing about this is your not tied in to a long term contract so if it fails you can try something else, if it succeeds you can adapt your strategy, and get a cheaper longer term rental or purchase payment plan for your truck to lower costs.

A good alternative to the food truck is the pop up restaurant, its a very cheap and quick way to test. Unfortunately this is not popular in every city so the food truck might be more reliable.

You can test out different locations with different demographics if you dont get off to a flying start or the footfall was lower than you expected. You can test different time frames, an example would be catering to night life rather than your usual day time trading. You can observe which of your meals are not finished and try to improve the recipe or swap it out for something else. You can change the outward appearance of your food truck to make it more inviting. You can change the name of the truck if its confusing or you find something better. You can even change the whole concept again and again until you hit a winner. Test, test, test, test, test thats why the food truck is such a great opportunity.

NUMBER 23 -

VENDING MACHINES

This is a very passive business and can be worth your while, if you can get your machines into the right places. The vending machine business has branched out in to many different niches from toys to coffee, viagra, pizza, sweets and even gold bars in some very affluent places of the world.

Dont be afraid to change your product or your location if you are not making many sales. You can literally pick up your business and take it somewhere else, which is an unbelievable advantage you have over other business types. You can even change all the products in your machine for something else until you find your eventual winners.

A good way to test quickly is to put a different product on each and every section this way you get to see the winners and the losers much quicker, all you have to do then is double down on each winner and drop the losers for something else and continue the process.

Ask your self this question, does my vending machine and the products match up with the customers needs and wants in this time and place. You can sell toys at a creche for children and condoms at a night club but not the other way around.

Try to buy your machines second hand if possible to save some money and check for defects before making the deal.

Increase prices until profits decline, not the number of sales.

NUMBER 24 -

CREATE A CAR PARK

It's time to get creative, if you haven't got millions in the bank you're probably not building a car park or buying one.

Can you find large residential gardens close to the town centre that you can offer to buy? If you can strike up deals like this it should be fairly easy to get an investor to put up the money.

Speak to your council about change of use before buying, it's likely they will say yes if the area is crying out for a car park.

You can do the same thing with buildings that need to be demolished, Market places that no longer do business or use up the total space.

Earnings will vary by location, what you can charge for parking prices and the amount of car spaces you have available.

If there are fields next to a bootsale or an event where there is always trouble parking, try to do a deal with a land owner to manage his land as a car park as and when these events take place, I have seen people use this strategy and they are very busy every sunday. Im sure there are places that could do with this everyday of the year and people willing to strike a deal with you to run this type of operation. This could work really well for someone who has a huge driveway or field but is rarely home to take advantage of the opportunity that you can manage for him.

NUMBER 25 -

CANOE RENTAL

The little boat you can rent out for $15 per hour. Can you sell 67 a day and make sales of $1005 a day ?

Have you got a lovely river near you where restaurants and pubs are filled with customers that can be your customers to ?

You can do a deal with a business owner to have your facilities near or on his busy establishment.

The start up cost depends on how much you can buy your first Canoe for, ebay is a good resource for used canoes they start around $100 and go up into the thousands.

In the right area with the right climate this can be a fantastic business. The only expenses you pay are rental each month for docking and storage which you might be able to get around if you have your own facility to keep the boats and a position on the river which does not require you to pay anybody.

Most people dont spend a whole hour on the boats so you can get more than your hourly rate per boat sometimes.

This is a simple business if you can find the right locations, maybe you live right next to a place like we have described and the opportunity has been waiting for you to take advantage of what is right in front of you.

NUMBER 26 -

AMAZON KINDLE PUBLISHING

Can you write a book, have you already written one and can't get it published ?

Why not try publishing directly to the Amazon marketplace and partner with the biggest retail company in the world.

If you don't think you can write a book you're probably wrong, no one finds it easy to write great books. It's often said the first draft is for the bin, so keep trying.

If you cant write stories or help other people tell their life stories, you could try and write a non fiction book like you are reading now. You can research all the information you need online or at the library and compile a useful resource for your customers.

Be ready to earn anywhere from $0 to Harry Potter Money, its likely to be closer to $0 if your being honest with yourself but thats ok. You don't have to stop with your first book and it doesn't have to become a full time job for you.

There are lots of tutorials and courses on how to write all different types of books so you can take advantage of all the people who have already taken this path. There is nothing better than taking action and looking for ways to improve your skills, no one becomes a master in a day, so keep training.

Amazon will print your book on demand when you get a sale, and digitally publish your ebook and audio books to their platforms.

NUMBER 27 –

MOBILE PERSONAL TRAINER

If you're a personal trainer and can create workouts that don't really need lots of equipment, you can train people in their homes and gardens charging more per lesson than the usual gym trainer.

Not everyone wants to go to the gym and deal with a hundred random strangers each time they work out, so there are people that would prefer working out at home. It even saves time for people commuting to and from the gym, and makes it possible for people with dependants to get a personal trainer without having to leave someone who needs them at home.

The accountability of having a personal trainer and the knowledge they have will keep you from procrastination and save you time getting towards your goals. They can also help you work around injuries that you have and avoid future problems.

This is a good way to start a personal training business without being controlled by a gym or having a large amount of start up capital.

If you can document your clients results you can use one of the greatest marketing plays by using pictures and video testimonials that prove your winning formula.

You should try facebook lead ads to gain some leads for your services.

NUMBER 28 -

WALKING TOUR GUIDES

This is good if you live in a historical area and a great idea for all the historians that left university without a job. This as a chance to pay off some of that college debt.

Firstly you need to find an interesting route with a lot of history, stories and visually appealing scenery.

Then we research everything possible about the area and the people that lived there. Now it's time to write the script full of great stories and golden nuggets of information to wow your customers again and again.

You repeat the same stories over and over again but everyone who goes on the tour thinks you'r a genius.

In london it costs around £20 per hour per person to take a guided walking tour, if you can attract ten people per hour you have a £200 per hour job.

The walking tour guide business is under attack by the tech industry which has many apps which offer audio tour guides that you can listen to on your phone. If you want to do this business to make some money,

I would do it within the next 5 years before it becomes the norm to use audio recordings as your tour guide.

I imagine augmented reality glasses will take a large part of the industry as well.

NUMBER 29 -
AMAZON FBA

Start selling your products on Amazon and take advantage of the biggest marketplace in the world. You send your products to Amazon and they pack, ship and provide customer service for these products.

I would do as much research as I could before I jumped in, and take a course that I can afford to invest in, there are some free ones out there but research the courses and read the testimonials. Some courses I have taken over the years have sent me down the wrong path, those courses were nothing to do with Amazon but the principle remains the same, do your research.

The free marketing you get from having your products on this platform should be enough to convince you of the opportunity available to anyone who masters this .

Amazon have more credit cards stored than any other retailer and they offer to deliver the next day for the vast majority of their products. You also benefit from the massive amount of trust their brand gives you when selling on their platform.

Amazon FBA is an amazing opportunity to get into, imagine you could get your products into Walmart or some of the other big retailers this easily.

This does not work out for everybody so please do your research and educate yourself.

Start up costs are around $3000 on average

NUMBER 30 -

TRAINING CENTRE

What skills, knowledge and techniques do people want or need to learn from a coach ?

Evaluate what types of training people are looking for then find an appropriate teacher to take the class if you cannot do it yourself.

Have some practice runs at the lesson before you start teaching to iron out any wrinkles you may have.

Try to cut the lessons up in to as many baby steps as possible.

Find a temporary place to hire out for your first experiment, always try to find venues that already have your target customers and use that to your advantage when marketing.

Set up work stations for your customers to practice their skills as you guide them through the process.

Each and every training centre is different and will require different equipment, insurances, space requirements and so on. Try offering the training which is the least elaborate first, then build from there.

When finding a permanent space, it might be good to make an offer to a business not advertising for rental and has never thought about renting, rather than just go for the offers already available. You could even do a profit sharing deal with the owner and have no fixed cost to cover.

NUMBER 31 -
SUBSCRIPTION BOX'S

If you have never heard of subscription box's they are monthly memberships where you are sent a box of products every month for a fee.

This type of business is hot right now and we will see many people become extremely successful with this business model in the future. The subscription model has always been a great option to have in your business.

One of the best examples of this is dollar shave club which sends its clients shavers each month. It's so simple yet so successful.

Some companies make random gift box's but most stick to a niche and send you related products.

Find wholesale products, possibly private label them or create your own.

Packaging counts for a lot so make sure to put major effort into making your unpackaging moments epic.

You can send your own packages at first then, when you start to make a lot of sales it is worth giving the packaging and customer service over to a logistics company.

Getting the customer to pay for the first month is always the hardest, so it might be worth selling the first month at an offer price to make the sale. If you break even the first month but acquire the customer on a membership basis, you still win.

NUMBER 32 -

ICE CREAM VANS

What a great little business ice cream vans, these can be great in the right area.

The profit margins are high for ice cream and ice drinks like slush puppies, there is an opportunity for you to earn a lot of money if you can find high foot fall areas where people are having fun. Parks, stadiums and theme parks come to mind when thinking about a perfect venue.

The weather in your location is obviously a massive consideration to take in, if it's not hot business is going to be slower.

The start up costs are the van which you can finance, around $700 of stock to start, tax and permits if needed. Its a good idea to have extra freezers in your garage for your stock.

Peoples food habits are changing to much healthier snacks but as of this moment the majority of people still love an ice cream on a hot day. And most health conscious people still treat their selves now and again.

Test locations, pricing, products and everything you can think of from the tune your van plays to the outward appearance and anything else you can think of.

Throw in some health snacks to get the other 20% of customers your missing, try everything.

Maybe you will end up with a fleet of ice cream vans like Alan Sugar did.

NUMBER 33 –

ATM BUSINESS

This might only be available in some countries so please look up your countries rules before wasting too much time researching this strategy. Or make your business in a country where it works and hire people to deal with the day to day operations and the problems.

You buy the ATM get it installed in a business location and get paid by the customers fees for usage.

This can work out well where there are lots of cash only businesses and the customers need to use your machine to get cash out.

The cheapest ATM machine I have seen is $2000 but is goes up to $16,000 and beyond. You will have to work out what is best for you in the long run.

You will also have to fill your machine with at least $500 and increase that overtime so you don't have to be constantly filling the machine and disappointing customers.

This is a good passive income strategy if you can get someone trustworthy to maintain your machines.

I dont know if this strategy will last forever as some countries have started to create laws against charging fees to get cash out of the machines. In the U.S.A its still ok, and im guessing it will be for a long time to come.

Do a lot research on your ATM locations and stake them out to see how many potential customers you could attract.

NUMBER 34 -

PRINT ON DEMAND

Create designs for T-Shirts, leggings, skateboards, hoodies, mugs and everything else you can think of that requires a graphic design.

Upload your images to a print on demand service where you can add your design on to products where they list them on their website, sell, print, package and run customer service for you.

The service providers are improving all the time and Amazon has started there own called Merch by Amazon there is Printful, Zazzle, Teespring and many other's with a slightly different take on the business model.

For graphic designers this is basically a free option to start selling products right away. Creating graphics with sites like Canva is really easy these days. If you dont want to create designs yourself try, 99designs, Fiverr and Upwork they can be cheaper than you might expect with quality that matches almost anybody.

Each service provider has different rules but im sure you can advertise the products yourself, with whatever means you have available to you for most of them.

If you have a social media following in a certain niche you can make products targeted specifically for them, and offer the products you know they will want.

NUMBER 35 -

FLIPPING HOUSES

Buying and selling houses for a higher price. Most people who do this try to buy the house below the average market value, renovate the house, make it beautiful and sell it on for a profit.

You can actually just buy houses that are below the market value and sell them on straight away for a higher price without doing any work, if the market value is higher than what you paid.

I have bought, renovated, rented out, sold properties and wish I had just flipped houses over and over again instead.

You can find houses like this just by looking on the property portals but the best deals will be the ones you find yourself, or you buy off property sourcing companies for a fee.

Try to do this in an area where houses sell quickly if possible, maybe there is an area which is hot with investors because of the regeneration happening there.

You can sell these on in no time at all.

Look in to the minimum value of a house that can be mortgaged in your country, this way you can find out what the smallest possible deposit will be in your country.

Some people use other types of loans to acquire property but I cant recommend them as they may require exceptional risk management skills and an understanding of the investment world that most people dont have.

NUMBER 36 -

EBAY

There is a lot you can do with Ebay for anyone to just get started. Firstly it gives you the chance to practice selling products you own but no longer want for a small fee which is paid after the sale is complete.

Ebay is known as an auction site but it is used just like any other ecommerce store a lot of the time using the buy it now feature.

Once you have sold all your unwanted things it's time to create a real business selling products from wholesalers either buying in bulk or dropshipping which is buying and sending products from a wholesaler after you have made the sale, and the product is directly sent to the customer from the wholesaler.

You can try buying and selling products you can find in places like flea markets, craigslist etc but it's not very reliable and has a very short term, labour intensive, hit and miss aspect to it.

One of the main things that makes Ebay so great is that many people are already comfortable buying and selling on the site, so its just a matter of finding good products and taking things to the next level by treating it as a business.

Ebay is still one of the biggest ecommerce sites in the world and its platform allows you to sell things with no marketing cost, and an easy set up process.

NUMBER 37 -

FENCE INSTALLATION

Installing fence panels in peoples gardens, it's not a glamorous job, it requires getting your hands dirty, a bit of upper body strength to move the fence panels around and the posts are heavy too.

The upside to this business is that it takes about an hour to learn, the tools to get the job done only cost around $100 and all the materials can be delivered straight to your customer so you don't need a large van to get started. A van will be worth getting, in the long run though as you will have bags of concrete and your tools getting dirty everyday.

The average installation cost of fencing in the U.S. is $2,388.

This is probably 6 hours work for 2 workers. You can get started on your next job that day and add 1 or 2 extra jobs into your weekly schedule.

You should add other services to your business so you can get over any void periods. Fence painting, tree surgery and hedge trimming are some great options to add.

The exercise benefits, and the outdoor lifestyle are extra benefits to consider on top of the money and a low tech simple business you can enjoy day to day.

You will want to set up google my business, a website and try google ads. If you dont want to deal with technology there is always leafletting, local newspapers and trying to get referalls from other companies.

NUMBER 38 -

FITNESS BOOTCAMP

There are a lot of these now, fat camps, body transformation, strength training and many more.

If you can find a niche that you can help people with your in with a shot. This trend is only going to get bigger so catch the trend before your niche is full of competitors.

Yoga camp, booty camp, Cardio camp whatever you can think of that has some demand.

You could start your first project/camp in a public space like a park to save on hiring a hall or gym. It depends on your specific training and the equipment needed to get results.

If your charging $99 for 2 lessons and you have got 10 students your sales are $999 and you could get a lot more students to attend.

If your training is of a good standard the word should spead fast, as the fitness communities are very passionate these days. Your social media presence could catapult your success if you do it the right way.

You should have a look at all the other fitness boot camps and try to emulate all the things they are doing well. Concentrate on your customers concerns and show them how you will help fix their problem or improve something by taking them to the next level of their fitness goals.

NUMBER 39 -

ASSISTED HOUSE SALES

This is a cool strategy for making money in real estate without much start up capital and some will and skill to renovate houses.

Firstly you need to look for houses selling at a low price due to not being renovated and within your price and skill range to repair. Of course you dont have to be doing the physical work but you will need to understand how much it will all cost to refurbish and the potential unseen problems that can occur.

You need to approach these home owners and try to arrange a deal where they take their house off the market while you renovate, decide on a price that the property would of sold for, if it did not get renovated, so you can split the increase in value once its sold, minus the cost of refurbishment.

Get an assisted sale agreement contract from a specialist property lawyer.

If you can communicate this strategy in a simple way to your potential customer you should be able to strike a deal that really benefits both of you and sounds like a no brainer to your lead. Make sure to emphasize how you will use a property lawyer to write up the contract and have his lawyer look over the simple document.

This really is a win-win business model that lets you get into the property game for the price of renovation.

NUMBER 40 -
PODCASTING

Have you listened to a podcast it's just audio recordings or live video streams of people talking, and its now one of the biggest mediums of entertainment in the world.

Everything goes, Chatting with your entertaing friends, Interviews, lectures, comedy hours, even just commentating on other events in a certain niche, its all up for grabs in this new world of entertainment.

The great thing that people love about podcasts is that there is no time limit on how long a podcast can run so conversations have more depth and you can get into detail about subjects that were really only dicussed at a very shallow level on television or radio. Another thing that is great about the format being audio is that people can listen to it as they are working on something else, driving, travelling on the train and just walking around.

This is bigger than radio now and anyone can start for a few hundred dollars or less.

The main platforms are itunes, spotify, google play music, stitcher and tunein.

Its worth uploading to youtube and facebook and any other platform you can find.

When your up and running there are many monetisation strategies to take advantage of, sponsorships, adverts, selling your own products, patreon, selling each episode, etc. Why not give this a try for the fun of it.

NUMBER 41 -
CAR WASHING

If only your parents taught you how to clean these properly and told you to charge at the market value for your services. Maybe your whole life would have turned out differently.

A sponge, bucket, cloths and car shampoo is enough to get started. Can you find $10 to start a business that works every time ?

Dress like a pro and get business cards on vista print or a similar site to add some professionalism and credibility in the future, but get started with what you have even if its nothing.

The prices for this service vary a lot, starting at $10 and going up to $50. High end detailing of luxury cars can be in the hundreds.

Cheap first time Offers, add ons, and bundles take this business to the next level.

Watch all the instructional videos you can after your days work to pick up tips, find new tools and products to improve your service and speed up your process.

Add other income streams to your service like small repairs like leather car seat repair etc and any other related service you can offer that will make your business more successful and profitable.

NUMBER 42 -
FOOD CART/STAND

This is like a smaller version of the food truck business, you will have seen hotdog stands, ice cream stands maybe a coffee stand and so on.

Is there a fast food concept that requires only a little space for preparation and cooking that you want to try.

You can get a stand for around a thousand dollars, you will need stock and maybe a permit to sell in your place of choice.

You can test different types of foods, different areas, pricing strategies, meal deals, the look of your cart, your clothes, etc.

Find out what works, buy your next cart and hire your first employee's.

Some food carts make as many sales as the restaurants around them, but they only have the one employee and little to no expenses when compared to a full restaurant.

Would you rather have a nice big restaurant with lots of employees or a few food carts making you the same profit. If your only after prestige I guess you will take the restaurant, if you can get past your ego and do what is simpler and more logical you take the food carts for an easier life with no contracts, less staff and fixed costs to worry about.

Your scaling stategy is just $2000 reinvested in the next food cart in a new area.

NUMBER 43 -

MEAL PREPARATION SERVICE

Can you make someone a tailored service to save them time and help them enjoy every meal by preparing their meals for the week and having them readily available.

How much do you earn an hour and how many hours of meal prep do you do per week ? Are you losing money by making your own meals ? that is a good question your customers can be asked in your marketing efforts.

You can concentrate on a certain niche such as weight loss, muscle gain, mexican food, italian food, etc

The Price per meal prepared varies and it will require research to get your pricing right.

This trend is only going to get bigger as people get busier and have more expendable income.

How much more time would you gain back per year if all your meals were prepared for you, how much healthier would you and your family be, what would you look like, how would you feel, how many memories would you have made in that time you gained back just by using the meal preparation service, would you look forward to eating rather than just going through the motions.

This is the type of message you can use in your marketing efforts.

NUMBER 44 -

SIMPLE TEMPLATE APP

This is not developing your own app from scratch or hiring programmers and coding your own app.

This is simply using the template apps available on many template sites where you simply add your information and images into the template you want.

You can make fitness plan apps, quizzes, games, chat apps and almost everything else you can think of,

Over 25% of IOS apps earn over $5000 per month and 16% of Android apps do the same.

A low barrier to entry, good branding and user satisfaction all help your success.

Many apps these days have paid and free versions, the free version usually has advertising or is a limited service unlike the paid version.

Some apps have in app purchases to make extra money, a lot of the games have features like these some being controversial like features making the games easier to win in an online setting.

Whatsapp used the stategy of giving the product away to the customer for free for the first 12 months then charged them a small fee.

NUMBER 45 -

SOCIAL MEDIA FLIPPING

Social media flipping is the process of buying, improving and selling social media accounts for a profit.

You can buy these accounts on sites like flippa.com, fameswap.com, etc If you buy multiple accounts you can advertise your other accounts to gain more followers, which has the effect of making all the accounts more valuable.

If you can see a way to improve the social media account by looking at what has already worked for them and doubling down on creating content similar to their most popular content you should increase your following.

You can outsource all the work to a social media manager, you will want to get samples of the work before you agree to any contract. You find these types of employees on upwork, fiverr and other similar sites.

There are lots of ways to monetise these accounts by selling shoutouts, affiliate products, your own services or products, etc If you have a business and you are looking to improve your presence, you can buy a social media account within your niche and use it to your advantage rather than selling it on. Its not flipping but it is building.

NUMBER 46 -

DOG WALKING

This is another business that costs almost nothing to start, maybe you will have to buy a pack of plastic bags to pick up the dog mess for $2 and then it is just a matter of knocking on doors to get started.

You probably have a bunch of friends who would pay you to walk their dogs, so reach out on social media, put up a facebook page and start getting customers with no advertising cost. Look at pet fan pages you can post in as well.

How many dogs can you walk at the same time? . In the U.K. it is now illegal to walk more than 4 dogs at a time, and you will get a £100 fine.

The average dog walk for an hour is $20-40 per dog, if your walking 4 your making $80 to $160 per hour which is not bad for a walk around the park.

Weather will effect your business so take that into account, if you live in a place that is always raining you will lose more days work than most people.

Towns like Manchester in England have a lot of rainy days so dog walking is less profitable there than Miami, Florida where most days are dry. You cant fight the weather so make sure you have other sources of income if you live in a place where your work will be called off all the time.

Buil up a dog walking round then get your first employee.

NUMBER 47 -

ESCAPE ROOMS

This is a trend that has increased in popularity over the last five years. If you don't know what it is, escape rooms are a new form of entertainment where you search for clues and solve puzzles to gain your freedom from the escape room.

If you have ever watched crystal maze it gives you an idea of what you may encounter.

You will need a physical premises and some decorations and props to make the experience interesting and exciting. Audio and visual equipment, insurance, etc

The average price per ticket is $25 and 10-12 players are usually allowed to play in any one game.

Your escape room premises does not have to be the most glamorous location as windows are not necessary and could actually take away from the experience.

This gives you the option to rent out the least desirable low priced commercial unit and make something great out of it.

Think of themes rather than just puzzles to entice your new customers into booking a ticket, movies, historic periods in history, low tech, pirates, vampires, sci fi, horror, countries, comedy, popular culture etc Make your puzzles a mix of physical and mental tasks to gain the next keys and make sure the first keys are not to difficult so people enjoy the experience, increase difficulty later.

NUMBER 48 -

SELF DEFENCE CLASSES

There are many different types of martial arts to learn, mixed martial arts, boxing, tae kwon do, jiu jitsu, krav maga, marine corp martial arts etc You don't have to be the expert or be involved in any classes, you can cut a deal or employ a teacher to train the students. You will need to hire a hall and have all the equipment needed for your lessons.

You could consider doing boot camp style trainings, taking people from total beginner to gaining some competence within the shortest period of time, so that they feel comfortable in a self defense class for the rest of their life.

The prices vary massively, a monthly subscription usually costs around $50 and one off lessons can cost the same so do your pricing research.

The martial art you practice is not the only niche you can seperate into, some people target a niche type of customer, for instance there are women and childrens self defense classes all over the world but there are other niches you could try catering to. The elderly might like to take classes, as they become more fragile and fearful as they age, knowing techniques that limit damage to them is a noble service for the elderly.

MMA and Jui Jitsu are the trending classes of our time.

NUMBER 49 -

HOLIDAY LETS

Could your home be a good holiday home for tourists, how much does you local hotel charge for a weeks stay ?

People will pay you a similar price to stay in your holiday let, if its at the same luxury level as the hotel.

You can use a platform to get bookings using sites like Airbnb, VRBO, clickstay.com etc

Check out your competition on the previously mentioned sites, to get an idea.

When you take your next holiday you can rent out your own home and have someone pay you for leaving your house.

Rental income varies by location and individual property massively.

Maybe its cheaper for you to be on holiday in another country rather than live in your house. That could be a good problem to have, its one of the advantages of living in an expensive country that you probably have not considered.

Tourist locations are the obvious safe bet when it comes to holiday lets but dont count yourself out just because you do not have Disney on your door step.

You can test this with your own home, and if your renting you could even ask permission from your landlord.

NUMBER 50 - CONSULTANCY

What knowledge do you have now or knowledge you can find and organise that people would be willing to pay you for ?

The information does not have to be stored in your head and communicated to your customer at a moments notice.

Arrange a time to speak to your customer on your schedule and ask what questions he would like to address on the booking form.

This gives you time to prepare and research anything that you are not sure of, or consult someone else yourself.

Find your areas of expertise and gather as much information and resources on your niche subject as possible.

Your service will improve with each customer you get and every question you encounter so dont be to hard on yourself when your first starting out. If you dont feel you have given your customer a great service and it bothers you, there is always the possibility of giving them there money back.

Consultants charge anywhere from $50 to thousands per hour. The price does not vary just by industry and subject matter but by by your prestige and status within the industry, the price your willing to set is up to you, so test, test, test.

This is another service business you can start today.

NUMBER 51 -
COLLECTABLES FLIPPING

This is a little bit like antique flipping, so if you have seen the antiques road show you will have an idea of how it works for the antique dealers, who often buy the antiques they are shown and sell them on for profit.

With collectables flipping we are looking at things like autographs, signed letters, classic cars and other types of interesting items.

There are websites where you find these products for sale which specifically sell certain types of collectable.

You can buy items that are in demand for collectors from sites like ebay and anywhere else you can find them, Maybe create a valuable group of products and sell them at auction specifically designed for that niche for a great profit.

Presentation counts, many signatues you see are just written on a piece of plain paper but use a full glossy image of the person above. This is made possible by using picture frames with a small section at the bottom meant for a few chosen words to be written.

The sum of the parts are more valuable than the individual parts on most occasions. A good example of this is having the signatures of all the Astronauts or a classic sports team on one large frame with all the signatures presented at the bottom.

NUMBER 52 -

CLEANING COMPANY

This is a great subscription business to start, with a high chance of success if you have some business sense and can hire and grow the company.

Your starting point, buying all the cleaning materials for your first job, then going from house to house or small business to small business offering your services.

You can create a facebook fan page, google my business page, social media accounts, and a website all for free.

If you get a job for a larger company with a massive office don't panic and hire freelance cleaners to help until you can justify hiring employees when you get your long term contracts.

If your starting this business as an individual and want tips on cleaning fast and with great results, look to youtube and read blogs on the best products and best practices of cleaners all over the world.

You can offer one off cleanings as well, for landlords and anyone else who needs a one off service, but always concentrate on trying to sell those subscriptions.

This is another simple business that has made lots of people millionaires just by scaling their services from town to town.

The average monthly subscription costs $150-260 for cleaning once a week.

NUMBER 53 -

CAR RENTAL

You can rent out your own car using one of the apps available to make some extra money and get a feel for what its like to rent your car out and what it entails. Look at what these companies have to do for you to rent out your car so easily with insurance arranged and so on.

Doing this on a bigger scale seems expensive and daunting but you can try starting with one car you buy with financing and try to rent it out for a reasonable daily rate.

If your car is different to the boring cars people can hire for a similar rate you could get more bookings than expected. Even hiring out cars for a purpose like having your other car fixed can be used for some enjoyment factor. I dont know why all the car hire businesses use such boring cars, they should have novel cars that excite the client and charge a premium to hire them out. Maybe they have a good reason, I imagine they get good deals on purchasing multiple vehicles that did not sell well for the car manufacturers.

Look into the laws for this type of business as closely as you can and find all the best practices of the industry to avoid any pitfalls associated with lending out your cars. I imagine public indemnity insurance is a must, and making sure the drivers take out their own insurance is just as valid.

Lets say your monthly car payment and insurance is $350 and you rent out the car for $35 a day, you need ten days booked to break even.

NUMBER 54 -

ONLINE COURSE

Can you create a course that can help people, you probably have acquired some knowledge or skills over your life time and someone will be willing to shorten the learning curve with your tutorials.

The courses don't have to be massive 30 hour courses and takes years to make.

Check out some of the courses on Udemy and other similar sites to get some inspiration.

You can host the course on your website if you don't want to use one of the platforms, where there is obvious competition, pricing wars, and platform restrictions.

When making your course, cut the video tutorials into easily digestible lessons so it's easy for your students to understand and progress.

Some people use whiteboards to teach, some just talk, some do demonstrations, some use screen capture software, everyone does it different so dont get too stuck on the technical aspect and deliver your content in the way you think is right.

Courses sell from 0 to thousands of dollars. Businessmen are used to taking courses that cost thousands of dollars to learn a new skill, Its cheaper than college and you can actually learn things from people that use the skills everyday.

NUMBER 55 -

DRIVEWAY RENTAL

Do you live in congested area in a big city where parking spaces sell for massive amounts of money.

Can you strike up deals with household owners in big cities like London to help them rent out their parking space to city workers ?

There are apps already available to parking space owners like Justpark, Parklet, etc but you can arrange yearly rental agreements with city workers and present this to your parking space owner without using an app.

When you get permission from the car park owners to rent out your space, you can go to your solicitor and get them to write up a contract for you, the space owner and the person who rents it out. You can print these out and use them over and over again.

To find people looking for a long term parking spaces call into offices near by and ask if you can advertise on their internal email sent out to all employee's.

Long term car rental is a privilege in big cities where parking spaces cost hundreds of thousands to buy sometimes.

Depending on the position of your parking you can be making anywhere from around £200 a month in london to £0 if there is no demand for your car park.

NUMBER 56 -

WEBSITE CREATION

With all the tools available these days setting up a website is a hundred times easier than it was ten, fifteen years ago. Wether you want an ecommerce store, a blog or just a site for your business there is a simple template available if your willing to look for it.

The price to have a website created by someone else has become cheaper but it's not a hundred times cheaper and you can make websites in hours rather than weeks so everything has worked out about the same for most developers.

The tools for creation are usually free now so all your costs for fulfilling your service costs you nothing, if you already have a laptop. Even if you dont have a laptop you can probably use a friend or family members for a few hours a day.

Some of the most popular website creation sites are wordpress, square space, wix, shopify, clickfunnels, weebly, gator, big commerce. They all have a slightly different take on the formula, I would use shopify for an online store, clickfunnels for direct marketing a product line and wordpress for the simple website for blogging or simple information like a businesses details and images.

The average cost to use a web developer in the U.K. is £2000-£8000 which gives the developer some healthy profit margins.

I dont know if this opportunity will still be available in 10 years time. The internet gets easier to use every day.

NUMBER 57 -

A MOVING COMPANY

If you have moved house and used one of these services you know its one of the bigger expenses of moving, and not an exceptionally difficult task to perform.

What do you need to start, a truck, some lifting dolly's and some reliable people to help move all the box's and furniture without damaging your clients property.

You or your employee will need the correct driving licence to drive a truck and you will need insurance to cover any damages.

Leasing your truck can can cost from around $1000 to $2500 per month. You could choose to rent out a Uhaul for the day which is good value at around $20 for a really short journey. To buy a new truck will cost you around $25,000 to $100,000 depending on the class of the truck. Look into second hand trucks that meet your criteria and if possible take a mechanic with you to look it over before purchasing and negotiating.

This company works better when connected to a large population in an expensive city where jobs come and go, circumstances change quickly and people have to make big decisions like moving to a small town to save money and commute to work, or transfer to another place with a lower cost of living.

In state moves cost on average $2300 and a long distance move usually costs $4300 on average.

NUMBER 58 -

A SANDWICH ROUND

This is a simple business opportunity that you can start from home.

You can start without a food truck by getting orders from offices at first and delivering the meals to the office with your sandwiches and other products in cool boxes.

If you can get large offices to order from you, it will be a great business.

Early morning preparation is one of the downsides of this business, if your'e making everything from scratch.

You can buy your products from bakers and just be the middle man to make things easier, when your only selling a low volume it might work out only slightly more expensive to purchase. Your energy will be better spent on trying to get orders for your products rather than worrying about controlling the manufacturing process at first.

Have the bakers wrap your food in your beautiful high quality packaging so you can sell the sandwiches at a premium, gain trust and have less skepticism about your products.

Your cool boxes should look professional as well so find some nice looking ones then add your logo with a quality sticker.

Pricing, volume and branding for decent profits make all the difference.

NUMBER 59 -

UPHOLSTERING FURNITURE

Changing your fabric, fixing springs and re-stuffing can cost almost as much as getting your new sofa.

The customer gets to have furniture that completely matches everything else they have or even just have something totally unique that no one else has.

The typical cost for refurbishing a sofa costs $700 to $1200 so this can add up if you have a lot of furniture to upholster.

Its easier than you think and it pays better than you would expect, considering the time it takes someone with experience to actually do the work on modern furniture, it's really a good business.

Have samples of lots of different materials available to your customers and picture or video examples to show them how the work might look when completed. Also let them know you can find materials to match the colour scheme and patterns already used in their home.

The skills and tools to start upholstering are widely available, cheap products and online tutorials are there to help you learn what you need to do within days.

Try looking for workshops in your area where you can learn all the skills needed in an enviroment you can get instant feedback from.

Your work is your catalogue to impress future clients so keep pictures and use these on your websites, social media and ads.

NUMBER 60 -
BUY TO LET

Buy a house and rent it out, this has made so many millionaires that it can't be dismissed.

The main strategy, find a house below the market value in an area with high rental demand and tenants that actually pay you. I would recommend buying with a mortgage to get the most leverage on your money.

Renovate and improve the property if you have the time to add value. Remortgage the property once you have improved the property and increased the value to pull your original investment money out and go again.

Check the laws in your city concerning when you can remortgage and all your legal requirement's.

The rental income should pay for your mortgage and return profits to you, make sure to keep some back for taxes and repairs to your property that you are responsible to pay for. Also consider the possibility of your property being empty and having to pay for your mortgage and council tax while its vacant.

House price increases over time and rising rental prices gradually increasing over time is where you will prosper in the long run, as the mortgage payments remain the same.

House prices usually double every 10-15 years so you make the equivelant of the full house price over this time.

NUMBER 61 -

WINDOW CLEANING ROUND

This is a great business to start as there is little to no start up cost and you can just start knocking on doors and offering your services.

If you don't know how to wash windows watch a youtube tutorial and become an expert in 2 minutes.

A ladder a squeegee, bucket, cloths and your ready to start, although there are more elaborate set ups that can be used and stop you having to climb ladders which is a really dangerous thing to do on a daily basis.

On average window cleaning costs from $2 to $7 per window pane. 20 panes costs from $40 to $140. Pick your location wisely! You could earn a fortune in a third of the time.

Get the right insurance to cover the possibility of falling for you and your employees. Window cleaning is one of the most dangerous jobs in the world due to all the falls of ladders that occur.

Dont just drop the leaflet on the door if possible, knock on the door introduce yourself give them the card or leaflet and explain that your starting business in this area and your ready to work whenever they need you. Get people comfortable with you so they will just call you when they need cleaning next time. People work with other people they know, like and trust.

This business can be started as soon as the sun rises.

NUMBER 62 -

MENTORSHIP PROGRAMME

Do you have years of experience to pass on to someone, can you look over their shoulder to train and guide someone, save them the years of struggle that you have endured to get where you are today.

This is a given for entrepreneurs who want to pass the torch on to the next generation and create responsible business people in the future.

Maybe your protege will be buying one of your businesses from you in the years to come, or partnering on a business opportunity with you.

Mentorship can be achieved in many different ways, the more intimate the relationship the more you can consider charging. You cant expect to charge as much for an email once a month as face to face mentorship once a day. On the other hand you can serve more protege's by answering questions by email once a month, but the value per person will decrease.

How much would you pay to save ten, twenty, thirty years of struggling rather than thriving at a young age when you have your healthiest years, how much would you pay to save your children from a lack of opportunity in their childhood. Mentorship is expensive in the short term but so cheap in the long term that it could save you a life not lived.

Mentors charge all different prices based on their perceived value to the student.

NUMBER 63 -
BUY A BUSINESS

Buy a business and skip the first dark ten years of a start up.

Do your due diligence and avoid the lies of many people trying to sell their business to you. Get a specialist lawyer who has completed on many acquisitions to help your journey go smoothly.

You can buy businesses with very little to no money down if you know what you are doing and can take over profitable businesses that will give you life changing amounts of income.

Cash flow needs to cover the debt, and the equity portion can be raised in many ways.

You can find businesses by directly approaching companies or using brokers, there are many platforms like daltons and businessforsale.com that help you find your first business through a broker. Using linkedIn to find your target businesses and ask if they have thought about selling or do they know someone in the industry who is, could be a place to start.

You need to study how to acquire businesses and have guts and determination to get a purchase to completion. You will have to approach a lot of businesses to offer deals and even when you find one that looks good on paper you will often find out that it is not what the owner made it out to be.

When this happens either negotiate for what its worth or just walk away.

NUMBER 64 -

RUBBISH REMOVAL

A simple business you can start straight away if you have a van or truck, if not lease one to start out.

Your'e going to be removing a lot of mattresses, stoves, sofas etc so get your self some dollies and other lifting machinery that can help you lift heavy objects everyday and avoid injury.

Home advisor say that the typical removal, costs between $135 and $375, a full truck full of rubbish costing around $500.

You will need an employee or a business partner to start this yourself as many of the tasks involved require 2 people to lift things like sofas and other large pieces of furniture.

This can be a dirty and labour intensive business where you dont look like the most successful person in the world. This can be a great advantage to you as it stops many people from starting this type of business and the less competition you have the better, this works especially well in the more affluent areas where telling your neighbors you own a rubbish removal company might be looked down upon.

If you can get the bookings and earn yourself $1000 a day with one truck, you will be earning more than most politicians and other professionals by providing this service to your community.

NUMBER 65 -

NICHE CATALOGUE

If you're selling to a niche group of customers by buying data or just targeting a type of housing that has your customers living there.

If your customers are the over 55's you can easily target your catalogue for the ageing population to these types of housing developments.

I know this type of marketing can seem old fashioned but it can still work for the right niche and work alongside your online stores.

Fill your catalogue with products from your wholesalers, hopefully you will be able to dropship a lot of the products so you don't have to buy a lot of inventory.

To keep your expenses down and test the viability of your catalogue you could test a tiny booklet of the best products you have to offer and only send out 100 at first, it's not a great sample size but it's a start if your low on funds. You might not get a statistically correct response the first time but it gives you an indicator of how much you should risk and wether you will want to increase the volume of catalogues on your next attempt.

Have your catalogue made by a graphic designer and present great products to your target customer who will want and need your great offers.

NUMBER 66 -
TOILETS

Yes there is money in toilets, wether its a paid public toilet or the hiring of portable toilets. Portable toilets are the lowest price option for you to start with then once you have built up you can try renting containers with full facilities including showers inside.

You can acquire a space in a public building and ask for permission to create a paid toilet facility, where you charge for the entrance fee. If you have been to Waterloo station in london or Liverpool St station you will have experienced this.

Renting out and maintaining portable toilets for festivals and other types of events is an option, but events usually only last for a few days.

The rental of portable toilets and other facilities to construction sites is more stable, most construction jobs can last months or years and lead to more contracts being signed with companies for their next projects.

This is a rental business with a customer base that will always be there, the demand for toilets will be here for as long as the human race. You cant say the same about many business opportunities.

This business will not be taken up by many people who have other options, its a great rental business and I cant see it becoming saturated with new people getting into the industry.

NUMBER 67 -

SOCIAL MEDIA MARKETING

COMPANY

You can help small businesses get leads and improve their online presence in a multitude of ways.

Most companies that have been around over 15 years and are not large corporations have little to no online presence, and if they do, it's not very successful anyway.

If they want more leads you can set up a clickfunnels site for them or a facebook lead ad. Create a website, facebook fan pages and instagram accounts to increase their brand image.

You can create a new ecommerce store with their products available, upload their inventory to Amazon, Ebay and Etsy.

Help create a subscription service for their products using Shopify or Amazon.

If they teach or consult you could help them make an online course and sell it on their website or a platform like Udemy or skillshare.

The upside for the business owner is so huge in some industries that the couple of hours a month looking after their ads and making sure they get new customers is a massive win for them, they are happy to pay for the service as the return on investment is so great.

You can charge anywhere from $1,000 to $10,000 just for running ads and creating content.

NUMBER 68 -

CREATE AN EVENT/ORGANISE

EVENTS

If you have good organisational skills you can hijack other peoples popularity and skills to work for you by creating events that help get performers on a platform to deliver their message, music, training or any other type of value they can deliver to your audience.

Starting out with something small like a town hall or a small event room in a hotel. Find speakers/entertainers at a level where they are easy to book and a venue thats easy to pack out.

You can sign up and sell your tickets on stubhub, eventbrite, etc Ticket collectors, Sound guys and helpers all add to your overall costs.

Ticket sales, Merchandise, Courses and food catering all add up to making great profits.

Set up your event in an area where you know your target market already exists and be focused on providing the experience that they really want as best as you can.

Use the speakers lists of fans to get some tickets sold for free and then drive traffic using facebook ads to your website or platform where you sell your tickets.

Scale up to selling out crowds in stadiums.

NUMBER 69 -

BOAT PARTIES

How do you make party goers pay through the nose to come to your party with an unknown DJ and a low end sound system, you hire a boat.

You can hire a boat on Boatbound which is like the airbnb for boats, make sure you have permission to have a lot of guests onboard and comply with all the rules.

In places like Ibiza you can sell your tickets for around 50 euros and get 100 to 200 on the boats that they use. Of course it all depends on what type of market you go after and what you offer, you could go after a higher end client and cater to that market.

If you go after the high end market you can sell the higher priced, higher profit services and products and make 3 times the money for the same or similar effort.

If you dont sell the last tickets you can call some of your friends or give them away to help advertise your boat parties. You want to make sure the boat is full up with party goer's to improve the atmosphere.

This is a business where you can make money having a party everyday, obviously its still work and responsibility but the pay and the perks make up for it.

A DJ, Boat driver and bar tender could be great business partners.

NUMBER 70 -

AFFILIATE MARKETING

Affiliate marketing is where you sell other peoples products and services and take a portion of the profit from the sales.

This is probably where most people should start and finish there careers, if they are not going to build up assets and ownership of businesses and houses.

Big companies like Amazon and Walmart have affiliate programs giving you the chance to sell world class products and services.

Most online courses have affiliate programs with very good terms like 100% commissions for your first sale.

The companies usually give you marketing materials, and many other resources like promo videos to help you. Some companies provide free training and support, run competitions have facebook groups and do things like live feeds and have meet ups for their affiliates.

Maybe you already have an online business with a great product that would benefit from having an affiliate programme where marketers make sales for you.

Having your own affiliates is like having a highly incentivised sales team, and if you are lucky you will attract some amazing affiliates you could of never hoped to hire.

Affiliate marketing pays well for the skilled and pays nothing to the amateur, so work on your marketing skills.

NUMBER 71 -
MYSTERY MURDER

Do you like the theatrical ? Have you ever wished you could be in a Agatha Christie story and be guaranteed not to die. These murder mystery weekends tick all the box's of the thriller novel readers fantasies and you can get paid to create it.

You can hold your murder mystery event over a weekend if you have enough accommodation facilities to cater for all your guests or you can hold these events for just the evening entertaining your guests for only a few hours.

Meals are usually not included but are offered as an option which adds to your total customer value.

I would look into who has the best reviews online and attend the top 5 competitors on their best evenings to observe and replicate the best features from each company. Many good owners and managers continue this practice throughout their careers.

You can base your evenings on a crime story novel that is interesting, frightening, clever and not so well known in popular culture that everyone can guess what will happen next.

The usual price per ticket in the U.K. is £50 and group sizes range from 7-200 people for large venues.

Look into the most entertaining aspects of live shows, deliver great dialogue and create moments that make jaws drop.

NUMBER 72 -

NARROW BOAT RENOVATION AND

RELOCATION

If you own your house, would you like to drop it in a town where it's worth a lot more money, like London, and sell it for a nice profit ? Well you cant, but you can do the same with narrow boats which are the cheapest place to live in most big cities.

I just gave you gold! but let's move onto the next part.

Renovate the boat you have bought, and make the inside a home, not just a boat.

Make sure you can get a mooring in the place you need to move to.

Get someone experienced to help you move your boat and learn from them, be careful and dont fall in a lock.

If you are looking for a property in a city location to live in this is probably the cheapest option after renting and your living space will be made to your specification.

There are other larger boats that are wider which might be worth looking in to as well.

You can even buy boats that are purpose built for full time living that are made to a high spec and still only cost about a quarter of the price an equivalent flat would cost you in London.

NUMBER 73 -

COPY WRITING

Copy writing is where you help companies and other types of organisations get more customers and sales with your creative writing skills.

You can use sales copy that is already in use that has had great success and adapt that to the company you are helping and their needs, with out plagiarising the previous work.

Most copy writers keep all the great copy writing they read from other writers in files to learn from and even copy from parts of their sales scripts.

There are many resources where you can learn about copy writing, books, online courses, local teachers and free information on youtube and other websites.

You can learn a lot from your competitors in the industry and see who is coming out on top, this gives you clues to how your audience is responding to different advertising offers and what you need to focus on and avoid.

Try to create a great story that connects the customers life with the product or service your offering.

You are basically selling the benefits of a product or service and trying to hit this home to the audience at an emotional level.

You can get paid thousands per sales letter.

NUMBER 74 -

PRIVATE DETECTIVE

Private detectives help individuals, companies and law enforcement agencies with tasks like helping find missing people, doing background checks and research for all types of crimes.

You should look into wether you need a license to practice in your state or country.

Do as much research as you can into all of the legal requirements you will need to fulfil to keep yourself on the right side of the law.

Private detectives charge anywhere from $40-$100 an hour with the national average being around $50.

You will be assisting the police with cases or working directly for your client.

Sometimes when the police give up on a case private detectives are hired by citizens of the public to continue work on these cases.

Staking out places, interviewing suspects and eye witnesses are all realities you can expect to be tasked with but the majority of the work will be behind a desk and using all the resources the internet provides.

This has the potential to be an interesting job and business, no 2 days can possibly be the same, you will end up with loads of stories to tell at parties where you will have to change the names of the people involved.

NUMBER 75 -

ECOMMERCE STORE

Your own online shop, this should not be your first option for selling things online as its easier to sell on Amazon, Ebay, Etsy, etc but it is usually cheaper once you have built up an email list and long term customers.

Unfortunately getting sales is more expensive as you will have to run ads and your conversions will more than likely be lower because your business is not as trusted as the previously mentioned companies and their platforms.

Try google shopping ads, then google search listings then fb ads in that order for pay per click ads.

You can find products from wholesalers, just google suppliers + the niche you're interested in. Try to use U.S. suppliers if possible. Or the country you choose to sell in's suppliers, this cuts down on shipping times and other problems.

I think Shopify is the best way to create an ecommerce store at this moment in time, it has made the process of creation so much easier and has lots of apps to help you improve your stores capabilities.

If the product and the offer is great everything else should be less difficult. Ecom is simple but not easy.

Use multiple well trusted payment providers on your site to help put your customers mind at ease.

You can lose money or make millions with this business.

NUMBER 76 -

BINGO

The house always wins! it's time for you to become the house. Don't be a gambler, be a business man and win every time you play the game.

You can find free bingo card generators for your games online, so that is a good start for making your games.

Has someone got a venue that has your target market already there waiting for someone like you to turn up and make a game for them. You should ask yourself this question for any location based business.

How much you charge per card and the prize will be factors in attracting customers to games and selling more cards per game, so experiment with it at different venues.

Bingo is widely loved and not taken as seriously as some of the other gambling games, I think that is because you can only buy so many cards and cant really spend like crazy which is a problem with certain games and sports betting.

Entertainment venues in holiday camps and tourist locations are good places to try out your first test run.

Bingo is an easy win if you have the right location, cheap venues and a large population of senior citizens.

NUMBER 77 -

MEMBERSHIP WEBSITE

Membership websites have a lot of advantages as a business model, as you only have to pay for ads to capture your customer once but you continue to get paid month by month, also your content is digital and is usually less costly to create than a physical product.

Great examples of membership sites are netflix, xbox gamepass, E-harmony, Spotify, and you can find many others of smaller size in niches you have never heard of still making great profits month in month out.

Have you got something to offer people on a recurring basis or can you collect other peoples creations to give to your customers.

Many of the best membership sites make none of their own content or very little in comparison to the vast amount of content that is provided by third parties. With services like dating sites you have to make the profile and become the content, that consumers pay to see. Streaming services mostly just pay other movie companies to place their content on their platform.

I bring this up so that you will take the time to think of different types of memberships and leverage other people's creations as well as your own and even let the customer be the creator on your site and charge them for the privelige.

$7 a month to your 1000 loyal fans is $7000 a month.

NUMBER 78 -

HOUSE OF MULTIPLE OCCUPATION

Turn your house or a rental property you own or will acquire into a HMO.

This is where you rent out your place by the room rather than renting out the whole house on a monthly basis.

It will be in your best interest to create as many extra bedrooms as you can splitting the living room into more rooms is a very common idea when creating HMO's and making large bedrooms into 2 smaller bedrooms.

Make sure to look into your local council's rules for this type of housing.

You have to take care of the small communal facilities that you provide and getting a cleaner in once a week is usually a good idea.

There is usually more turn over of tenants in a HMO, so be ready to fill the rooms quickly when someone leaves to get over any void periods.

Student lets can be a great thing if you live near a university. You can market to foreign students and have them pay the years rental upfront.

Depending on the house, how many rooms you can get in and the area that you live, you could double your rental income.

NUMBER 79 -

WHOLESALE BUSINESS

This sounds way more daunting than it should when you consider how small you can start.

You will need to rent out a storage facility of an appropriate size with parking for customers and enough space for the trucks to deliver products to you, before you put them up for sale.

Start in a small niche so you can work with a smaller section of the market, and work your way up to supplying the entire industries products.

Find a sustainable niche that needs constant re-orders then find manufacturers and wholesalers in your own and other countries that you can trust.

I recommend starting small and doing as much research as you can on each manufacturer/wholesaler.

Make sure there is a need for your product and then order your bulk items to sell to your retailers.

This is a simple business with thin margins and high volumes, you have to make sure retailers really want your products and that they will have a good chance to sell them.

Simple every day products make the wholesale business a lot more predictable and sustainable, but you can try your hand at what you think is the right industry to serve.

NUMBER 80 -

GARDENING SERVICES

This is a great business to start up as the skills are easily learned, it's an ever green business so your going to be able to hold off technological advances better than most types of businesses.

The other upside is that you can keep reasonably fit and strong doing gardening, with the added benefit of working outside in the sun light getting your vitamin D from the sun.

You will actually have a small chance of staying away from computer and phone screens the majority of the day which is a big deal for some people.

You can list your services on an app like mybuilder, checkatrade, ratedpeople, tooli, taskrabbit.

You should also condider trying craigslist and gumtree type websites for some cheap advertising.

Make sure you set up your google my business page, a website and facebook page, instagram is even worth a shot if you can deliver great images of the gardens and short videos.

Work on getting business through referalls by making deals with other companies that work at peoples homes.

The hourly rate and pay by service needed ranges drastically, £30 an hour is about the average in the U.K.

NUMBER 81 -

BOUNCE HOUSE RENTAL

Rent out air filled bouncy castles to people for their children's parties.

Is this an under served business in your area, if it is you could really have a great business to start up.

The average day rate for renting a standard bounce house is around $100 to $250 and the price to buy the bounce houses is getting cheaper.

You could start off your business with a smaller bounce house for around $300 but I would recommend getting a really stand out bounce castle for at least a thousand dollars so you can attract more potential customers.

When marketing, what do we ask ourselves ? Where is my target audience and who already has my customers ?

The answer to the previous question is fairly simple, schools full of children and other childrens entertainment venues like adventure playgrounds. You can offer the school a referall reward for every customer they send to you by using their email list.

Companies that organise parties could be a perfect partner for helping each other find more business. Card shops that sell hundreds of birthday cards every day are worth advertising in as well.

Google my business will be vital to your success.

NUMBER 82 -

FACE PAINTING

Sell your face painting skills and deliver your services in a multitude of locations, children's parties, night clubs, festivals, school fetes, halloween parties, theme parks, zoo's, creches, children's adventure playgrounds, etc test different events and locations to see which works best for you and your business.

Who already has your customers ? Schools, Children's party organisers, party decorators, etc find as many as you can to try and do deals with them for referrals that book you and possibly shared marketing opportunities.

Face painters average around $90 per hour for parties, some having a 2 hour minimum booking time as well.

Most face painters only do face painting and dont add on any other services within the party and entertainment industry they are in. For example, if you are face painting at a festival you can sell glow sticks and other items to your customers. You can rent out a bouncy castle and face paint while the party is going on etc.

Make sure you keep up with your customers changing tastes and watch the trends to get more bookings. If your doing face paints for 80's cartoons at a childrens party your not going to be very popular, so keep up with the latest trends and give your customers what they want.

Employ face painters and make this a business

NUMBER 83 - FURNITURE UP-CYCLING

This is a renovation type business where you buy or take peoples old furniture away for free! and create something new and fresh with what you have.

The simplest way to up cycle is to find great furniture that looks out of fashion and undesirable because of the colour and changing it with a paint or stain that is popular right now. You might want to change the handles etc for something nicer.

You can watch endless tutorials online and tv shows where people do similar things, to get some great ideas of whats possible.

Sometimes you don't have to change a thing and just need to find the right auction or platform to sell your furniture at a profit.

Etsy and other online auction sites are great, but high end and niche auctions lead to bigger profits! The niche websites are great because that is where the collectors of those certain items go and compete for their prized posession.

High end auctions like Savills and Christie's are usually catering to the affluent and items can sell for prices that dont make logical sense.

You can sell your products in a high end shop if you do a deal with the owner.

NUMBER 84 -

EXPENSE REDUCTION

CONSULTANT

Get paid to save individuals and companies money.

Build up strategies, systems, communities, resources, product and service lists, etc to save your customer money over time.

One good tip can save an individual thousands and a big company millions.

You can sell your service with a money backed guarantee, you save them a thousand or their money back.

Entice customers to send you their details with a set of question helping you see wether you can save them money before you start the process.

This way you never have to pay out on the guarantee and always help your client.

This is such a great service, can you imagine how many businesses you save and how many jobs your creating, your probably saving marriages as arguing about money is the number 2 cause of divorce.

The biggest expenses a business has are employees, rent or a mortgage, marketing and advertising for most companies, if you can find cheap and effective alternatives it can really help someone.

Expense reduction for individuals is usually so obvious and easy, if they have the guts to show you all their accounts.

NUMBER 85 -

SMALL BUSINESS COACH

If you have already made small businesses that are successful and you want to help the other entrepreneurs out there, you will love this.

If you can get the right business coach its like having a mentor at the same level but he is always concerned about pushing you forward and helping you change your company or project so it can be a success immediately.

The small business coach is being kept accountable by offering this service as a transaction, unlike a mentor who just helps you out at random times with less incentive to push you forward.

A lot of business coaches are always available by phone call, text or email and respond swiftly to help you solve problems as they happen.

The business coaches sometimes have contacts and resources that would not be available to you without their introduction.

If your trying to raise capital or get some type of deal over the line letting the people you are pitching to know your coach is always on hand to give you his counsel might help seal the deal.

This is a great business for someone who wants to help someone get ahead, and get paid. I love it.

NUMBER 86 -

MANURE SALES

Yes you can make money from other peoples crap.

Horse manure can be sold on as fertiliser for gardens and make you money.

How to get the manure for an extremely cheap price.

Start a stable cleaning service and get paid to take it away by the barrel load.

You will have to store the manure in an appropriate way and you will probably be able to do this on the property of one of your stable cleaning clients, for a fee. Manure does create toxic fumes, so you will need to take precautions and clearly sign the storage units as a toxic substance.

The stable cleaning business is probably a more profitable enterprise than the manure business but combined together they are more than the sum of their parts. There are not many businesses where you can get your product for free and get paid for it twice.

Shredded manure can sell for around $20 per 60L bag.

You will have to get advice on what types of insurances to take out, with the toxicity of the fumes and danger of working near horses you and your employees need to be covered.

This business takes the saying one mans trash is another mans gold to the next level.

NUMBER 87 -

COMEDY CLUB

The comedy club business is really the entertainment and momentary happiness business, usually with a bar and restaurant element added for an extra income source.

Is your town missing a comedy club from its entertainment and nightlife offerings ?

Does your area have enough talent to maintain a long term show for your customers, you will probably be surprised that it does, comedians are usually willing to travel long distances, it's a way of life for lots of comedians.

Think of a way to start with minimal cost like, hiring out an empty premises for the night or doing a deal with a restaurant that is set up well for entertainment, hire a small theatre etc.

There is probably a big city out there without one comedy club, There is definitely lots of large towns without them, which is just a shame, I would rather have a comedy club in my town than a night club, bar or theatre and I can't be alone thinking this.

The low ratio of comedy clubs to other entertainment venues creates a great opportunity and in my mind it's a kind of tragedy that we have no comedy clubs in some large towns.

Laugh your way to the bank, it will not be easy, but it might just be a dream worth living.

NUMBER 88 -

NETWORKING EVENT ORGANISER

This type of business has multiple different benefits to the owner, you can create an event that benefits your business, your hobbies or just meeting certain types of people.

Another benefit of owning and possibly hosting the events is that you become an instant authority figure amongst your community and will have close contact to the speakers and other types of guests you invite.

You have the opportunity of selling your other products and services at your events.

Eventbrite is a platform you can use to find customers and take payment for your events.

This gives you a chance to lead a multi faceted life around the multiple different communities, industries and hobbies you really like.

If certain days or times in your life are quiet and boring you can always set up an event and take charge of your life.

If one of your interests is in a very niche culture this is an opportunity to find and connect with those people.

You will make some money at the events but the real money will come from selling other products and services and a percentage of whatever the speakers sell while at your event. This can be about fun, money or both.

NUMBER 89 –

NICHE PRINTING BUSINESS

Starting up a printing business can be difficult so try and focus on a niche or multiple niches under separate websites.

Examples of printing niches include, high end business cards, personalised wall art, subscription box's, book cover's, shop fronts, product labels, warning signs, birthday and other types of cards, car stickers, laptop stickers and covers, leaflets, menu's, etc

Find your niche, look into the printing equipment needed and the rental terms, get a cheap commercial space or work from home.

Start an e-commerce site on shopify or hire a developer to create a site for you, if you want something more complex.

Start driving traffic to your store with google and facebook ads.

If your a great graphic designer this could be an option for you to capitalize on your talent and creativity.

If this seems like too much of a risk you could always try the print on demand services option first, test what works the best then decide from that point wether you want to make your own products for the printing industry.

The mark up on some print products is great if you can get the customers.

NUMBER 90 -
BATTING CAGE

This is a fairly simple business once its all in place, but there are still lots of things to consider before starting your first cages.

Is there a big fanbase of baseball and softball in my area and do they actually play the game rather than watching and talking ?

It is hard to tell if this will be successful so an experiment will have to take place, in order to be certain.

A batting cage can cost around $500 and a good pitching machine around $2000 so try to hire these if that is even possible where your based.

Find an appropriate place to rent a space, where your target customers are and the rental is a fair price.

Offer 1 on 1 training lessons, sell baseball merchandise on your shopify site and at your physical location, run day training camps, childrens parties, parties for adults where alcohol is served, try to get businesses involved by using your cages as a team building event.

Make you cage novel and interesting with metal cut out's of the villian's of history at the end, and try anything you can think of to make your cage stand out.

This business is another that is simple but not easy.

NUMBER 91 -

SPA BUSINESS

The spa business is another business in the service based business category which is becoming more and more popular as wealth grows across the world.

Has your country started on this trend ? This could be a great opportunity to create a massive business before the trend has become a normality in your country.

The services and treatments are so varied that you can decide on how much money is going to be needed, you could start with a massage table that you can take to someones home or you could buy machinery like floatation tanks and installations in buildings like steam rooms if you have start up capital.

You can build up to the point your that your business is really a Spa, Salon, Beauty treatment centre with a hotel attached, but you have to start somewhere and providing a service for the first time and hiring your first employee are big moments in any business.

Look at what others have done before and emulate the best of the best on your own budget and time frame.

The difference between the best and worst businesses in an industry can be the difference between looking after lots of small little details that can add up to success for you.

Differentiate yourself, Test Prices, Thrive.

NUMBER 92 -

CAR WRAPPING

Wrap cars with printed vinyl to change there appearance or even just protect the paint with a see through vinyl.

If you already have a garage this is a great extra business to add on, as you already have potential customers coming in each day to sell to.

If you don't have the skills to do this there are training schools around teaching this.

It can cost anywhere from $2500 to $5000 to get your car wrapped. The vinyl you will use starts at around $10 per metre and probably averages at around $20.

Keep in mind some vinyl will be significantly more expensive and the price of materials has to be passed on to the customer.

Differentiate yourself from other car wrapping companies with your own branded line of vinyl covers with your own unique patterns and colour variations made for an exceptional looking car you will not see twice.

Speak to vinyl companies to get your colours and patterns created for your private label products.

Use google my business to get started and make a website and facebook page.

Use the images and videos of your cars to put on your youtube, fb, and intstagram pages and send them to other people's channels, blogs, magazines etc for free PR.

NUMBER 93 -

HOME MADE FOOD DELIVERY

This is a trend that is only going to become more popular in the coming years, that you can take advantage of.

Some people are using apps like homemade to be the middle man for selling their meals and some are creating their own websites and only selling their own products.

Each business model has its merits and you may have to adapt over time as the consumers method of purchasing this type of service changes.

Test your pricing strategy and offer membership deals to retain customers over long periods of time. Win their loyalty and trust with your product and service.

Scale by hiring and creating Kitchens in commercial spaces strategically placed for delivery in your new expanded territory.

Dont always struggle to be number 1 in your area to squeeze out the last remaining profit, instead just concentrate on being profitable then move on to the next area that you can replicate your success in.

It's better to be the second best selling company in all the towns rather than the number 1 selling company in 1 town.

Build great teams, sell great products and let everyone know.

All you can do, is all you can do, and that's enough.

NUMBER 94 -

GOLF DRIVING RANGE

Do you know of a sports facility or even a golf course that has extra land but no driving range installed ?

You can rent or offer a piece of the profits to the owner of the land to let you install your driving range.

Some of the business can be automated with coin operated ball dispensers and most of the customers bring their own golf clubs. You only need one person to handle the golf club hiring job if you are not attahed to a golf course which already has this facility.

You will need a golf ball picker which is a retrieval device that is attached to the back of your golf cart. You can probably borrow a golf cart if your working with a golf course.

You can start with 1 station and keep adding stations as the money comes in, when you cant expand the practice stations anymore, you can add a restaurant and bar facility in keeping with your surrounding businesses. Once you feel you have a profitable formula for success start looking for your next location.

Look to the other successful ranges for ideas and inspiration and leverage all their years of testing to help you move forward.

The life time value of a customer can really be a life time, as golf is a sport you can do for life.

NUMBER 95 –

MINIATURE GOLF

These mini golf courses are becoming more elaborate and look like little theme parks that have way more novelty value than they had years ago.

Can you partner with someone who has the land and a large pool of customers looking for entertainment ?

The costs of starting the business will range massively based on how you want to start the business. You could choose to start with a very basic set up that only costs you less than $10,000 to get started then reinvest profits to improve each hole with expensive and elaborate show stopper holes to attract more customers.

The average price for a game is $5, but don't sell yourself short and test pricing.

If people can see your crazy but spectacular mini golf course from a busy road, its all free advertising. Your children are going to see this while you are driving in the car and ask to be taken there, it's so simple but it works.

If you try to make your holes based on a certain theme, make sure it's not something that will go out of date and need to be updated in the near future. You want an ever green theme like animals, pirates, space, countries etc this way you will have something that lasts.

Google my business, a website & a facebook page are advisable.

NUMBERS 96 -

LIFE COACHING

Are you a good example of a well rounded individual who has discipline in the major areas of your life, wealth, health, love and happiness.

Can you develop habit forming routines for your clients and help them use their personal values to motivate themselves into doing all the things they know they should.

You can't be an expert in everything and you will have to lean on different experts in all the necessary parts of life that your clients are dealing with.

Make plans, templates, routines, schedules, calendar's, Diaries, and have your students keep note pads to write out troubles that pop up each day.

Test what works for each individual client. No 2 people are the same and the cookie cutter approach to solving problems for people will not work everytime.

There are lots of psychological tests to evaluate yourself, there are therapy type exercises you can perform, there are tests to see what motivates you and many other tools to help you understand yourself.

Understand your clients, values, motivations, goals, first then come up with a starting plan, and adapt it to the revealed personality and nature of your client.

NUMBER 97 -

PERSONAL DRIVING SERVICE

Drive around business men and other important members of society while they carry on with their work in the back to remain productive and not add the extra stress of driving to their already demanding lives.

You will need the required licenses and a vehicle to get started, even though many of the clients will want you to drive their cars.

If your polite a good driver over long distances and don't have fits of road rage you could be cut out for starting this business yourself if funds are tight.

If you have a lot of money to invest you will be able to stand out with your vehicle line up from the start. You could even customise the interior to create the ultimate work space or specialise in another experience people are looking for.

Your cars could be adapted so you can have large tvs in the back with gaming consoles and internet services available to your client, so they can work or watch a streaming service or play a game between meetings, without using their laptop.

Send your offers to all the executives you can on linkedin and make videos explaining all the benefits of taking your offer.

Even just driving them to and from home in absolute luxury without the stress of driving in the city is worth it to a lot of people.

NUMBER 98 -

VOICEOVER SERVICE

Do you have a nice speaking voice that can be used for audio books, radio ads, online adverts for small businesses, movies and documentaries.

You can use platforms like Fiverr and Upwork to advertise your speaking gigs and upload examples of your work, which you can create before you even have your first paying job.

You can hire a studio by the hour to work on your projects or invest in your own recording studio if its within your budget and you have the space.

Im not sure how likely it is to have employees as voice actors without creating your own content rather than offering it as a service to book writers, and other content creators.

All I know is that there are millions of books out there that need someone to voice the audio versions and your company could provide that service and more.

Go direct to the authors of books and other content that do not have audio versions available and offer your services to them.

Could you be the go to service for all creators that need professionally crafted audio, who could not hope to create something as great themselves.

This is a good side job, maybe a business and has the possibility of a big pay day if you are smart or lucky!

NUMBER 99 –
PROPERTY MANAGEMENT

This is nothing new, not that clever, but difficult in some ways as you have to deal with hundreds of tenants day in day out, with all the problems that housing comes with.

You will also have to chase tenants for their rental payments and twist the arm of the rare landlord that does not want his repairs made in a timely fashion.

This can be a great business if you live somewhere that has a large rental population and does not have too many competitors in your local market.

Your usual charge for the management of a rental property is around 12% of rental per month, so if your customers rent is $1000 you get $120 for your management fee and there are other fees for acquiring tenants and doing checks.

The obvious other income source can be selling houses, which despite all the changes in recent years with online estate agents is still a very profitable business.

Other not so obvious sources of income can come from things like property investment training, having a renovation company that offers a deal to anyone who purchases a property through your estate agency and carries out the repairs for all the properties under management.

If you invest in property yourself, you will get to see the best deals come through your door first and get to buy them.

NUMBER 100 -

GUTTERS CLEANING AND FIXING

If you're not scared of getting dirty and afraid of heights this is a possibility for you to take advantage of.

Most of the gutters installed today are made of plastic, click together easily and are light and easy to carry.

The biggest expense you will have is your ladder, if you already have a van or a car of a decent size to carry materials.

You will need a good insurance policy to cover you in case of injury.

The average price for cleaning gutters in the United States in 2018 was $150 so its another service based business worth considering. Having your gutters cleaned does not take very long, maybe just over an hour for a detached house.

If you live in an area with massive trees your going to be extremely busy every fall, with your much needed service.

You can add exterior painting to your services as you are going to be encountering houses with stains over the front of them continuously.

If you have a window cleaning round this is a great add on as your already in position to work for your customer.

Set up your online presence and get referall business from all the other tradesmen you can find for a small fee.

NUMBER 101 –

BUSINESS START UP BOOT CAMPS

The business start up seminars were first started as an antidote to expensive franchises that left the owners with ever decreasing returns due to higher fees from the owners of the parent companies.

The way the start up seminars differentiate is, training you to follow a business system for days to weeks, then you are left to go out and start a business on your own terms with no one else dipping into the profits.

These seminars go over all the business basics and the practical skills needed to get started and show you how to scale from there.

You will be provided with templates and documents, video training, audio training, and more to support your daily practices.

These seminars can be very expensive, sometimes in the tens of thousands, but pay off for the attendees if they have the will to take action on what they have learned while attending.

Have you got a full business system that you can sell to up and coming entrepreneurs who need your help ?

If you can do this there is a lot of money to be made by making this accessible to people who were in your position

Give someone the help you wish you had when starting out, and get paid to do it.

THE BIGGER PICTURE

It all looks impossible.

When you look at a large business with lots of employees, offices, vehicles, a recognised brand name and millions in profits, it looks insurmountable.

The truth is they were all built brick by brick, baby step by baby step, mostly with people of average intelligence, performing tasks that a trained 15 year old could perform.

You can have a grand vision but your better off concentrating on performing a small action towards an easily attainable goal.

Even big business is mostly an illusion of grandeur, a suit, a logo and the rental of an office in an impressive building adds up to the impression that everyone knows what they are doing.

And yet big companies in industries that seem solid fail because they cant follow simple principles.

Find something you can understand, at least in the financial sense and make sure it will not be disrupted by technology and change to the point of destruction.

Start with a small experiment, maybe trying to get a customer before you even have a service or product to deliver. For services you can use a calendar and fill it up a month ahead, with products you can use a pre-order page or take emails to notify the release of your product.

Most service-based businesses require no start-up capital, and any money you need for most businesses can be raised in a multitude of ways, as long as it makes financial sense to the lenders.

If giving away equity is the only way to raise enough capital then so be it, having some of something great is better than having all of nothing.

Start your service with as little land, labour and capital as you can but no less.

This is usually called the minimum viable product which is another way of saying low cost experiment.

Insult your own intelligence and work on a business that seems below your capabilites first time out.

Create templates for all operations, systemise, create processes, build a team that lives by these and a manager for the team.

Scale by creating the next team in another location you have decided should be your next target.

Do what you can with what you have got, success is not based on how many resources you have, but how resourceful you can be with what you have.

You are always one decision away from changing your life, I hope this book gives you the courage to do whatever it is your looking for.

Martin Luther King:

"Take the first step in faith, you dont have to see the whole staircase, just take the first step"

Good luck in whatever you decide to do, make your dreams come true.

Thank you for reading.

Scott McDowell

Document Outline

- <u>STARTING A BUSINESS</u>

- <u>NUMBER 1 - WEDDING PLANNING</u>

- <u>Number 2 - POWER WASHING</u>

- <u>NUMBER 3 - CARPET CLEANING</u>

- <u>NUMBER 4 - WOOD FLOORING SANDING AND
  POLISHING</u>

- <u>NUMBER 5 - PET GROOMING</u>

- <u>NUMBER 6 - CAMERA MAN/VIDEOGRAPHY</u>

- <u>NUMBER 7 - INTERIOR DESIGNER</u>

- <u>NUMBER 8 - PARTY DECORATOR</u>

- <u>NUMBER 9 - PEST CONTROL</u>

- <u>NUMBER 10 - PERSONAL ASSISTANT SERVICES</u>

- <u>NUMBER 11 - CHILD CARE</u>

- <u>NUMBER 12 - TREE SURGEON</u>

- NUMBER 57 - A MOVING COMPANY

- NUMBER 58 - A SANDWICH ROUND

- NUMBER 59 - UPHOLSTERING FURNITURE

- NUMBER 60 - BUY TO LET

- NUMBER 61 - WINDOW CLEANING ROUND

- NUMBER 62 - MENTORSHIP PROGRAMME

- NUMBER 63 - BUY A BUSINESS

- NUMBER 64 - RUBBISH REMOVAL

- NUMBER 65 - NICHE CATALOGUE

- NUMBER 66 - TOILETS

- NUMBER 67 - SOCIAL MEDIA MARKETING COMPANY

- NUMBER 68 - CREATE AN EVENT/ORGANISE EVENTS

- NUMBER 69 - BOAT PARTIES

- NUMBER 70 - AFFILIATE MARKETING